TIMELINES OF
AMERICAN HISTORY ™

A Timeline of the War of 1812

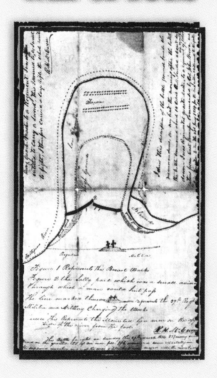

Sandra Giddens and Owen Giddens

The Rosen Publishing Group, Inc., New York

Published in 2004 by The Rosen Publishing Group, Inc.
29 East 21st Street, New York, NY 10010

Copyright © 2004 by The Rosen Publishing Group, Inc.

First Edition

Library of Congress Cataloging-in-Publication Data

Giddens, Sandra.
A timeline of the War of 1812/Sandra Giddens and Owen Giddens.—1st ed.
   p. cm.—(Timelines of American history)
Summary: Provides a chronological look at the activities in the United States and abroad that led up to the War of 1812, as well as events of the war itself.
Includes bibliographical references and index.
ISBN 0-8239-4542-1 (lib. bdg.)
1. United States—History—War of 1812—Chronology—Juvenile literature.
[1. United States—History—War of 1812—Chronology.]
I. Giddens, Owen. II. Title. III. Series.
E354.G44 2004
973.5'2'0202--dc22

                                     2003016714

Manufactured in the United States of America

On the cover: The Battle of New Orleans during the War of 1812 is depicted in this undated engraving of an original painting by Dennis Malone Carter.
On the title page: Diagram showing the position of American troops at Horseshoe Bend on the Tallapoosa River, Alabama, where General Andrew Jackson put down an uprising during the War of 1812.

Contents

1

The Reasons for War

Wars are rarely fought for only one reason. Rather, there are many causes that precede the decision to enter into a planned war between nations. The act of war is not an immediate response. The War of 1812 was a means to settle arguments that had been simmering

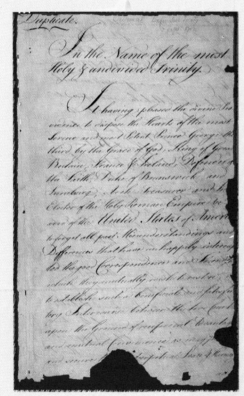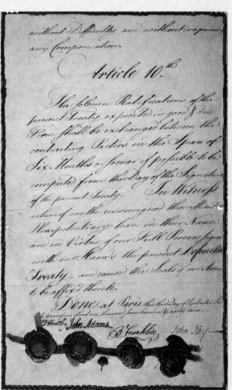

Treaty of Paris

between Great Britain and the United States since the end of the American Revolution in 1783. When these arguments finally came to a boil between the two nations, the War of 1812 began. Its battles were fought on both land and sea from June 1812 to the spring of 1815.

★ 1783

Great Britain and the United States sign the Treaty of Paris, thus ending the Revolutionary War. The treaty indicates that the colonies, now known as the United States of America, are free. The treaty does not define the border between the new United States and the British colony of Canada, however. The British promise Native Americans that they will remain in control of the Ohio River Valley. Many Americans are eager to gain territory and begin settling these lands, anyway. Soon, a conflict over the Ohio River Valley begins.

★ 1789

Tecumseh, a brilliant leader, respected warrior, and skilled speaker, leads war parties against the American settlers.

Tecumseh, a Shawnee chief and resistance leader, was killed in 1813 leading Native Americans in an uprising against American forces during the War of 1812.

Native American Resistance

Americans who pushed into Native American territories paid little attention to treaty borders. They completely disregarded Native American land claims. Some angry Native Americans

Tecumseh defends the British while on horseback in this nineteenth-century print. The Native American leader's influence against the Americans was felt most during the capture of Detroit in 1812.

turned to their British allies for help. British officers and traders listened sympathetically to their complaints. In exchange for furs, the British gave guns and ammunition to Native American warriors, knowing these weapons would be used against American settlers. In the years before the War of 1812, two influential Native Americans were the Shawnee brothers, Tecumseh and Lalawethika (Prophet). They led war parties in an attempt to defeat American settlers. There were great losses on both sides.

6

★ 1789

George Washington is elected first president of the United States. The French Revolution, prompted by economic depression, high taxes, overpopulation, food shortages, and a rising national debt, begins in France.

★ 1791

Arthur St. Clair, the first governor of America's Northwest Territory, takes his 2,000 untrained troops and tries to fight the Native Americans. He is defeated and 900 of his men are killed.

General Arthur St. Clair was a British-born American colonist who had fought in the American Revolutionary War and served as a delegate to Congress between 1785 and 1787.

★ 1792

The French Revolutionary War (1792–1802) begins. American resentment of the French grows during this conflict. France dominates the continent of Europe, and Great Britain rules the seas.

★ 1794

Not all fights with the Native Americans end in failure for the Americans. Major General "Mad Anthony" Wayne and his American troops defeat the Native Americans at Fallen Timbers (present-day Toledo, Ohio).

Assault on the High Seas

While tensions increased on the frontier, the United States was also having difficulties on the high seas. Before the Revolutionary War, American ships enjoyed protection under the British flag, but following independence, the British no longer protected them. Pirates now assaulted American ships. The British wanted to keep American ships from reaching France, and the French had the same idea about blockading British ports. President George Washington established

Americans capture the British pirate known as Blackbeard in this eighteenth-century painting by J. L. G. Ferris. Blackbeard, also known as Captain Edward Teach, died in 1718.

the United States Navy on March 27, 1794. Congress was concerned. How could the United States fight on both land and sea?

★ 1795
President George Washington sends Chief Justice John Jay of the Supreme Court to Great Britain to negotiate a new treaty. The Treaty of London (Jay's Treaty) has the British agree to evacuate its forts south of the Great Lakes. British fur traders continue to trade on the American side of the border.

★ 1796
John Adams is elected president of the United States.

★ 1800
Thomas Jefferson is elected first Republican president of the United States.

John Adams (1735–1826), a Federalist, won the presidency in 1796 over Democratic-Republicans Thomas Pinckney and Thomas Jefferson, who became vice president that same year.

★ 1801
An American fleet carrying members of the U.S. Marine Corps cruises the Mediterranean to protect other American ships. The marines use rifles and grenades for protection. These Americans are remembered in the song "To the Shores of Tripoli."

2
The Embargo Act

France and Great Britain each claimed the right to seize ships bound for the other's ports. If neutral Americans traded with the British, they risked losing ships to France. If Americans traded with France, the British could take everything. Because Americans were making a fortune in sea trade, they continued to sail. In fact, between 1803 and 1807, profits from American trading went from $13.6 million to $107 million. The British practice of "search and seizure," the impressment

Artist Michele Felice Corné created this illustration of the bombardment of Tripoli in 1940 for *Life* magazine. It shows the U.S. squadron successfully shelling forts of the Barbary pirates in 1804.

(forced service) of seamen, was one conflict that led to the War of 1812. The British forced more than 10,000 Americans to work on British ships between 1803 and 1812.

1803

★ The British search American ships for sailors who desert the Royal Navy. Desertion is a problem for the British. The British navy pays less than a third of what American sailors earn. British deserters put themselves under American protection by jumping ship at American ports and taking out naturalization (citizenship) papers. British captains refuse to recognize these documents and instead force British-born seamen back into their service. Hero Lieutenant Stephen Decatur rescues 300 sailors in the harbor of Tripoli who were captured on the *Philadelphia*. The United States purchases the Louisiana Territory from France.

This document, written in the hand of Thomas Jefferson, is part of a collection of general correspondence related to the purchase of the Louisiana Territory in 1803.

★ 1804

President Jefferson is reelected.

1806

Americans believe that British impressment of American sailors is an act of aggression.

11

The Non-Importation Act

President Jefferson could not stop British search and seizure operations. In 1806, furious Americans supported the passing of the Non-Importation Act, banning British goods from entering American ports. France's Napoléon excluded British goods from entering Europe, hoping to further ruin British industry. The British responded with a blockade, seizing approximately 1,000 American ships. In 1807, after the British fired on the American frigate USS *Chesapeake*, Jefferson wrote the Embargo Act, which banned American ships from exporting U.S. goods to any foreign nation and devastated New England shipping.

★ **1807**
Three Americans are killed and eighteen are wounded when the USS *Chesapeake* is fired upon by the British. President Jefferson demands an apology from Great Britain but is refused. Jefferson attempts "peaceful coercion" of the British with his Non-Importation Act banning British goods from America. It is followed by the Embargo Act, cutting all trade with France and Britain. These laws create an economic disaster for American businesses. Thousands of Americans lose their jobs.

★ **1809**
James Madison is elected president of the United States.

The British fight American forces during the War of 1812 by sailing up the Chesapeake Bay to set fire to Washington, D.C., the new capital of the United States.

3

The War Begins

Native American Tecumseh and his brother, Prophet, founded a growing settlement in northern Indiana called Prophet's Town. William Henry Harrison, governor of the Indiana Territory, was nervous that the Native Americans would form an alliance with the British. He feared that Native Americans would drive the American settlers out of the Ohio River Valley with British help. In 1810, Tecumseh confronted Harrison and warned him that the Native Americans of the Ohio River Valley would give up no more of their land. Tecumseh's message to other Native Americans was that they must fight to get their land back.

★ **1810**
James Madison urges Congress to pass a new law. It promises that if either France or Great Britain lifts its restrictions on American shipping, Americans will resume the embargo against the other nation. France agrees and the Americans forbid all trade with Great Britain.

In this engraving, a British officer interrogates a group of seamen on an American vessel in order to determine if they had deserted the British navy. Americans were often forced into service by the British.

★ 1811

William Henry Harrison gathers his military a mile from Prophet's Town to divide the Native American Confederacy. After a surprise attack led by Prophet, Harrison's army of 1,000 men fight back in the Battle of Tippecanoe. The American army drives back the Native Americans. As a result of this battle, many Native Americans side with the British in the War of 1812.

The Battle of Tippecanoe, depicted in this print (*above*), took place on November 7, 1811, between American forces led by William Henry Harrison and Native Americans led by Tecumseh. The Native Americans were defeated at Prophet's Town on the Tippecanoe River in Indiana.

The War Hawks

Failing in peaceful efforts on land and sea, and facing an economic depression, some Americans argued for a declaration of war to restore American pride. In Congress, a group of Democratic-Republicans known as the War Hawks demanded that war be declared against Great Britain. These men argued that British policies could be changed by an invasion of Canada. The Federalist Party, representing New England shippers, foresaw the downfall of their trade and opposed war. Nevertheless, on June 18, 1812, President James Madison signed a declaration of war.

★ **1812**
President James Madison is reelected. The United States attempts three unsuccessful invasions of Canada. The USS *Constitution* ("Old Ironsides") defeats the HMS *Guerriere*.

★ **June 16, 1812**
Parliament suspends British laws against American shipping. Unfortunately, without fast communication devices, this news is very slow in reaching the American people.

James Madison (1751–1836) is referred to as the Father of the Constitution because he helped write *The Federalist*, a series of papers that pushed toward ratifying it. Madison was elected president of the United States in 1808.

The British navy aboard the HMS *Guerriere* attacks Americans aboard the USS *Constitution* ("Old Ironsides"), on August 19, 1812, in this painting. As the story goes, the badly damaged British ship attempted to bombard the Americans, only to find that the sides of the *Constitution* were made of iron.

June 18, 1812 ★
Without knowing the laws against American shipping had been suspended two days earlier, President Madison, pressured by the War Hawks, asks Congress for a declaration of war against the British. President Madison stresses "free trade and sailors rights" as the leading cause of the conflict.

4

The War Continues

America seemed strong. There were almost 8 million people in the United States compared with only a half million living in Canada. In reality, the United States was weak. The U.S. Army was small and scattered, and the militia was unreliable and poorly trained. The navy was also insignificant. Compared with Great Britain with its 600 fighting ships, America had only about 20 vessels and a few gunboats. The United States was not prepared for war.

★ **August 5, 1812**
Native American fighters led by Tecumseh kill 17 men out of a troop of 200 led by General Major Van Horne in the Battle of Brownstone.

★ **August 9, 1812**
Battle of Magagua. American forces are driven off by British forces with help from Native Americans.

★ **August 15, 1812**
Fort Dearborn Massacre. Potawatomi Native Americans attack American militia and civilians. Americans are massacred and taken prisoner.

R. F. Zogbaum painted this image of American sailors on the deck of the USS *Constitution* during an 1812 battle off the coast of Nova Scotia with the British ship the HMS *Guerriere*.

August 16, 1812 ★
American surrender of Detroit. The United States loses Fort Mackinac to invading British armies.

August 19, 1812 ★
Captain Isaac Hull's USS *Constitution* is defeated after sinking the British ship the *Guerriere*. The *Constitution* is nicknamed "Old Ironsides" and will become the most famous ship in the navy's history.

The Surrender of Detroit

American hopes of conquering Canada collapsed in the campaigns of 1812 and 1813. The initial plan of the United States was to invade their northern neighbor through Detroit, Niagara, and Lake Champlain. These attacks were uncoordinated, and they failed. During the second month of the war, General William Hull surrendered Detroit to the British. On the Niagara front, American troops lost the Battle of Queenston Heights in October. Along Lake Champlain, American forces withdrew in November without defeating enemy forces. Meanwhile, the British gradually tightened a blockade around America's coasts, ruining U.S. trade and exposing the entire coastline to British attack.

American army officer William Hull is seen surrendering to the British in this undated engraving. The Americans surrendered Detroit to the British on August 16, 1812.

In a decisive battle of the War of 1812, American naval forces under the command of Commodore MacDonough *(center)*, defeat the British on Lake Champlain. The American victory ends the British invasion.

January 1813 ★
Battle of Frenchtown. British and Native American allies defeat Kentucky troops. The American survivors are killed at the Raisin River Massacre.

April 1813 ★
Battle of York (in present-day Toronto, Canada). American troops take control of the Great Lakes and burn York.

American naval commander Oliver Hazard Perry defeats the British navy on Lake Erie, in Michigan (*above*), challenging British superiority in the Great Lakes during the War of 1812. Perry (*below*) is rowed to the *Niagara* after the destruction of his flagship, the *Lawrence*.

★ **September 1813**
In an important American victory, the Battle of Lake Erie, U.S. forces under Captain Oliver Hazard Perry defeat a British naval attack.

The Battle of Lake Erie

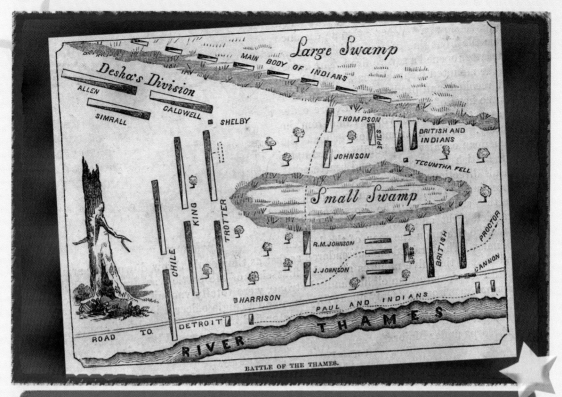

BATTLE OF THE THAMES.

This historical drawing (*above*) documents actions at the Battle of Thames in which American forces crossed into Canada via present-day Lake Erie on October 5, 1813. The British are defeated along with Native American supporters. Tecumseh (*below*) is trampled and killed.

Death of Tecumseh

October 1813 ★

In another important American victory, the Battle of Thames, also known as the Battle of Moraviantown (Ontario, Canada), Tecumseh is killed. His death ends the dream of a Native American confederacy and discourages his followers.

November 1813 ★

Battle of Autosse. Two hundred Native Americans are killed.

A Surprise Defeat

The United States seemed defeated. The British appeared successful by 1814, and, having defeated Napoléon, they turned their attention to America and invaded New York. General Sir George Prevost, with his 10,000 troops, moved from Canada to Plattsburgh on Lake Champlain. Although the British had a larger force than the Americans, they failed. The Americans surprisingly defeated the British forces. News of this defeat convinced the British government it was time to end the war.

Before being turned back during the summer of 1814, the British attacked and burned the U.S. capital. Although most of Washington D.C.'s residents had fled, First Lady Dolly Madison remained in the White House long enough to gather important national documents and the famous portrait of George Washington by Gilbert Stuart.

March 27, 1814 ★
Battle of Horseshoe Bend (Mississippi Territory). Andrew Jackson defeats Native Americans. The British plan a three-part invasion of the U.S.: Chesapeake Bay, Lake Champlain, and the mouth of the Mississippi River. The British are turned back at Baltimore Harbor. Francis Scott Key composes the song later called "The Star-Spangled Banner."

August 24–25, 1814 ★
The British burn public buildings in Washington, D.C., including the Capitol Building and the White House. Madison flees.

September 1814
Battle of Plattsburgh (Lake Champlain). The U.S. secures its northern border with a victory over the British.

December 24, 1814
The Treaty of Ghent is signed by British and American diplomats.

General Andrew Jackson (top), remembered for leading Americans to victory at the Battle of Horseshoe Bend during the War of 1812, later became president of the United States in 1829. The Treaty of Ghent (bottom) ended the War of 1812 between the United States and Great Britain.

The Treaty of Ghent

After the war with Napoléon, the British were sick of high taxes, high prices, and the loss of so many lives. The Duke of Wellington advised the British against further action in the long and expensive war in America. Finally, in Ghent, Belgium, British and American representatives began talking seriously about ending the war. On December 24, 1814, the Treaty of Ghent was signed. By January 2, 1815, the HMS *Favourite* sailed to America with a copy for ratification

The Battle of New Orleans, which continued after the Treaty of Ghent was signed and while word was being delivered to Americans about the war's end, is illustrated in this print. Two thousand British soldiers were wounded in the battle at the hand of American forces.

by the Senate and to get the president's signature. Meanwhile, the war continued in America.

★ **January 2, 1815**
The HMS *Favourite* sets sail to America.

★ **January 8, 1815**
Battle of New Orleans. Eight thousand British soldiers march on New Orleans. Andrew Jackson, who leads more than 6,000 troops, defends the city. American forces kill 289 British and wound 2,000 in the battle. The remainder flee. Jackson scores a huge victory and paves the way to the White House. The United States loses only 31 soldiers in the conflict.

★ **February 16, 1815**
Congress approves the Treaty of Ghent. The War of 1812 is over. Territory and prisoners captured by either side are returned.

★ **1816**
James Monroe is elected president; the Era of Good Feelings (1816–1823) begins. This period in U.S. history marks a time when Americans are anxious to forget political issues and international conflicts and return to normal life.

James Monroe (1758–1831), fifth president of the United States, is seen in this engraving.

27

Using Timelines to Show Relationships

Timelines show the relationships between events as they happened over a specific period. Occasionally, this information is condensed to include details about the events that may or may not have been included in other accompanying text. It is sometimes easier, even at a glance, to gain facts about events when they are shown in the order that they occurred. For instance, details about the individual battles that led to the end of the War of 1812 can be seen in a few short passages in this book. Events like the formation of the Embargo Act illustrate how situations surrounding the conflicts between nations erupted into a war. Timelines are especially useful in learning about history and its relationships.

Glossary

alliance (uh-LY-uhnts)   A close association formed between people or groups of people to reach a common objective.

blockades (blah-KAYDS)   Ships that block passage to ports by ships of another country.

colony (KAH-luh-nee)   A region controlled by a distant country.

Congress (KON-gres)   The part of the U.S. government that makes laws and is made up of the House of Representatives and the Senate. The members of Congress are chosen by the people of each state.

diplomat (DIH-pluh-mat)   A person whose job is to handle relations between his or her country and other countries.

economics (eh-kuh-NAH-miks)   The study of production and supply and demand of goods or services.

embargo (em-BAR-go)   A government order prohibiting the movement of merchant ships into or out of ports.

frigate (FRIH-git)   A three-masted sailing ship that carries its guns on a single gun deck.

frontier (frun-TEER)   The edge of a settled country, where the wilderness begins.

impressment (im-PRES-ment) The act or policy of seizing people or property for public service or use.

independence (in-dih-PEN-dents) Freedom from the control or support of other people; self-rule.

negotiate (nih-GOH-shee-ayt) To talk over and arrange terms for an agreement.

neutral (NOO-trul) On neither side of an argument or a war.

pirates (PY-rits) People who attack and rob ships.

treaty (TREE-tee) An official agreement, signed and agreed upon by each party involved.

Web Sites

Due to the changing nature of Internet links, the Rosen Publishing Group, Inc., has developed an online list of Web sites related to the subject of this book. This site is updated regularly. Please use this link to access the list:

http://www.rosenlinks.com/tah/waei

Index

A Timeline of the War of 1812

Credits

About the Authors: Sandra and Owen Giddens have written a number of books for Rosen Publishing. Sandra is a special education consultant and Owen is a psychotherapist. They have two teenage children, Justine and Kyle.

Photo credits: cover, pp. 7, 8, 13, 20, 21, 22 (bottom), 23 (bottom) © Bettmann/Corbis;. pp. 1, 9 © R. H. McEwen/Hulton Archive/Getty Images; p. 4 © U.S. National Archives and Records Administration; pp. 5, 10, 14, 15, 16, 19, 24 © Library of Congress Prints and Photographs Division; p. 6 © Historical Picture Archive/Corbis; p. 11 © Library of Congress, Manuscript Division; p. 17 © Francis G. Mayer/Corbis; pp. 22 (top), 25 (top) © Nathaniel Currier/Hulton Archive/Getty Images; p. 23 (top) © American Memory/Library of Congress; p. 25 (middle and bottom) © Corbis; pp. 26, 27 © Hulton Archive/Getty Images.

Designer: Geri Fletcher; Editor: Joann Jovinelly